**Scott, Foresman
Basics in Reading**

Daisy Days

Program Authors

Ira E. Aaron

Dauris Jackson

Carole Riggs

Richard G. Smith

Robert Tierney

Book Authors

Joanna Cairns

Elizabeth Galloway

Robert Tierney

**Instructional
Consultant**

John Manning

Scott, Foresman and Company
Editorial Offices: Glenview, Illinois

Regional Sales Offices: Palo Alto, California •
Tucker, Georgia • Glenview, Illinois •
Oakland, New Jersey • Dallas, Texas

Consultants

May Arakaki

Maria Eugenia Matute-Bianchi

Maria Bilbao

Delphina B. Briscoe

Deborah Flores

Jesse Garcia

Evangeline Geiger

Gordon Gray

Barbara Griffin

Barbara Hansen

Jerry A. Rainwater

Betty Robeson

Ann Semel

Joan Takada

Michiko Ikegami Totman

Evelynn Washington

Acknowledgments

pages 24 top and 27 bottom left: Miriam Austerman, ANIMALS ANIMALS

pages 24 bottom, 25 bottom, 27 top right, and 27 bottom right: Alan Nelson/Root Resources

pages 25 top, 27 top left, and 47 bottom: Zig Leszczynski, ANIMALS ANIMALS

pages 26 top left and 26 bottom right: Carson Baldwin, Jr., ANIMALS ANIMALS

page 26 top right: Ray Mendez, ANIMALS ANIMALS

page 26 bottom left: John Kohout/Root Resources

pages 39-44 We gratefully acknowledge the cooperation of the Docent Committee of the Lincoln Park Zoological Society and the Lincoln Park Zoo, Chicago, Illinois

page 46 top: Hans Reinhard/Bruce Coleman Inc.

page 46 bottom: Peter Menzel

Contents

Section Two

Section One

1

Context
Consonsants
Blend
Digraphs

Look and Listen

A dog and a frog had lunch under a chair.

A goat and a giant played with a green ball.

A sheep was washing a fish.

Think about skills

1. Does the letter *d* stand for the same sound in *dog, had,* and *under?*

If you said yes, you were right.

➤➤ Most consonant letters stand for one sound. This is not so if the letters are *c* and *g.* ◀◀

2. Does the letter *g* stand for the same sound in *goat* and *giant?*

3. Do the two consonant letters together stand for one or two sounds in the words below?

    played   frog   green

If you said two sounds, you were right.

1: Teach

» Two consonant letters together usually stand for two sounds. This is not so if the letters are *ch, sh,* and *th.* «

4. Do the letters *sh* stand for one or two sounds in *sheep, washing,* and *fish?*

Practice skills

Which word names the picture?

1. close house guess

5. play candy city

2. jet hit sat

6. pocket peanut present

3. bed bell but

7. camel circle candle

4. their car chair

8. sun sit six

LITTLE HIPPO

by Frances Allen

Little Hippo lived in the city zoo with his mother.

He had fun in his pond. He liked to make the children laugh.

1: Apply

But one day some workers came. They took
Little Hippo's mother away. And he was all alone.

That night Little Hippo cried.

The next day Little Hippo cried. He could not
stop crying.

"Why are you crying?" asked a ladybug.

"My mother went away, red thing," said
Little Hippo.

12

"I'm not a red thing. I'm a ladybug. I'm sure your mother will come back soon," said the ladybug.

"She's been gone a whole year," said Little Hippo.

"When did she leave?" asked the ladybug.

"Yesterday!" said Little Hippo.

"Look, here comes somebody now. Is that your mother?" asked the ladybug.

"Yes!" said Little Hippo.

"I'll say good-by. I must fly home to my children," said the ladybug.

"Look at the surprise I brought you!" said
Little Hippo's mother.

"A baby sister! Can she play games?" asked
Little Hippo.

"We will teach her some," his mother said. "And
you will never be alone again."

And he never was.

Think about the selection

1. What question did the ladybug ask Little Hippo on page 12?
2. What did Little Hippo call the ladybug on page 12?
3. What was the surprise for Little Hippo?
4. What question did Little Hippo ask his mother on page 15?

Checkpoint 1

1. Do you hear the r sound at the beginning, in the middle, or at the end in these words?

   yesterday   red   mother

2. Where do you hear the ch sound?

   teach   children

3. Where do you hear the k sound?

   back   came   workers

4. Where do you hear the s sound?

   city   yes   yesterday

Pete Makes His Plans

Pete the giant sat in his yard for a while. There was a nice breeze. He saw a bird. He liked her singing. But he had to start to make some plans to clean his house. He'd fix it so he had space for his pets.

Think about skills

» A vowel letter stands for more than one sound. Two vowel letters together usually stand for one sound. **«**

Words like *sat, pets,* and *his* usually have a short vowel sound.
Words like *make, Pete, clean,* and *while* usually have a long vowel sound.
Words like *yard, her,* and *bird* usually have an r-controlled vowel sound.

start   plans   breeze

space   bird   had

1. Which words have short vowel sounds?

2. Which words have long vowel sounds?

3. Which words have r-controlled vowel sounds?

Practice skills

Pete found a bird cage with a perch. He found five tan shirts. He had a scarf he didn't need too.

He put the things in a box and gave them to his sister.

shirts   and   five   perch

things   need   scarf   cage

1. Which words have short vowel sounds?

2. Which words have long vowel sounds?

3. Which words have r-controlled vowel sounds?

2: Teach/Practice

WHAT MADE THE TRACKS

Mari and her brother Tomi saw tracks in the clean
snow. They wanted to know what animal had
made these tracks.

First the children
followed the tracks down
the street.

Tomi saw the tracks by a
pile of sand.

Next Mari saw the tracks
by the side of a red car.

The children followed
the tracks into a park.
Tomi saw the tracks by
a lake.

Mari saw a bird in a tree.
She knew the bird hadn't
made the tracks. She
heard something behind
the tree.

Then out ran a big white cat!

2: Apply

Think about the selection

1. How did the Contents help you find this story in this book?
2. Why did Mari and Tomi follow the tracks?
3. How did Mari know that the bird hadn't made the tracks?
4. What made the tracks?

Checkpoint 2

tracks	these	lake	her	street
clean	first	yard	park	big
had	white	bird	red	next

1. Which words have short vowel sounds?
2. Which words have long vowel sounds?
3. Which words have r-controlled vowel sounds?

ANIMALS and THEIR TRACKS

Each of these animals makes tracks in the sand, snow, or mud. As you read, think of how the tracks of each animal might look.

This is a gull. Gulls live on the shores of lakes and oceans. They eat fish and other things. They have webbed feet with three toes in front and one in back.

This is a deer. Deer live in the woods. They eat grass and leaves from trees. They have hoofs on each foot.

24

This is a snake. Some snakes live in the sand near water. They eat toads and frogs. They have no legs. They move by gliding along the ground.

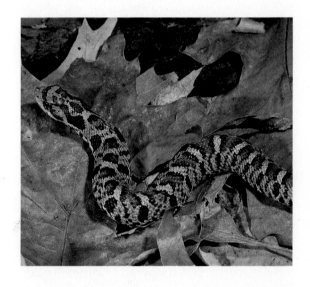

This is a raccoon. Raccoons live in the woods near water. They eat fish, fruit, and eggs. They have five toes with sharp claws on each foot.

Look at each picture carefully. Decide which animal made each set of tracks. You may want to read about each animal on pages 24 and 25 again before you decide.

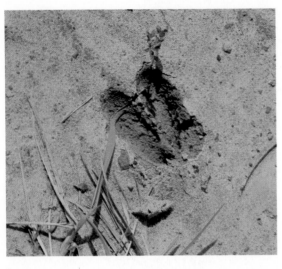

1

3

2

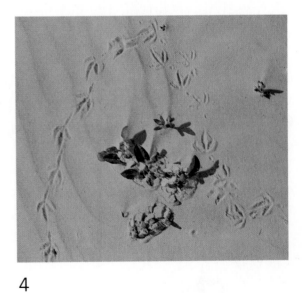

4

Think about the selection

a. snake

c. deer

b. gull

d. raccoon

1. Which animal has three toes in front and one in back?
2. Which animal has hoofs?
3. Which animal has sharp claws?
4. Which animal has no legs?

The Dragon Helps

A dragon once lived in a village near the ocean. <u>She</u> liked to play in the water.

One day houses in the village caught fire. The people were afraid. "What shall we do?" <u>they</u> asked.

"I'll call the dragon," yelled a boy. "She will help <u>us</u>," <u>he</u> said.

Think about skills

The underlined words in the story are pronouns. Pronouns can stand for names of people, animals, and things. The first underlined word is *she*. In the story, the word *she* stands for the dragon.

3: Teach

1. What does the word *he* stand for in this story?
   If you said the boy, you were right.
2. What do the other underlined words stand for?

Practice skills

The boy ran and found the dragon. "Will you please help us put out the fire?" <u>he</u> asked.

The dragon nodded. Then she swallowed a lot of water and blew <u>it</u> on the fire. The fire went out.

All the people were happy. "The boy and the dragon saved the village," <u>they</u> shouted.

"Thank you, dragon," said the people. "<u>You</u> were a big help."

The underlined words in the story are shown below. What does each word stand for?

1. he
   a. the dragon
   b. the boy

2. it
   a. the water
   b. the fire

3. they
   a. the boy and the dragon
   b. all the people

4. You
   a. the people
   b. the dragon

City Mouse and Country Mouse

One day a city mouse went to visit a mouse who lived in the country.

The country mouse lived by herself in a nest under a tree. Seeds and plants were all the country mouse had to eat. So she gave seeds and plants to the city mouse to eat.

The city mouse did not like seeds and plants. She asked, "Why do you live here and eat this food? Come with me to the city. There we can live together in a fine house. We can eat cakes and cookies and pies."

30

Late that night the two friends came to the house where the city mouse lived. They ran under the house and went through a hole in the floor. They came to a room full of good smells.

The country mouse found cakes and cookies and pie to eat. She said, "Oh, this is fine food. I'll never go back to the country to live."

All at once the city mouse saw two big round eyes looking at her.

"Run!" she shouted. "Here comes the cat!"

With one quick jump the city mouse went through the hole in the floor. The country mouse jumped right after her.

The city mouse laughed. "We got away from the cat that time," she said.

"Yes," cried the country mouse. "But see what the cat did to my tail. The cat got some of my beautiful tail."

34

The city mouse said, "When you live in the city you can't be so slow. You must be quick, or the cat will eat you."

"Oh," said the country mouse. "I will never live here. You have cakes and cookies and pies to eat. And I just have seeds and plants to eat. But fine food is not everything.

"It is much better to live a long time in the country than to live a short time in the city. Good-by!" said the country mouse.

So the country mouse went back to the country. And there she lived ever after.

Think about the selection

1. Find something the city mouse said in the story. Read it aloud the way you think she said it.
2. What did the country mouse eat at home?
3. What did the city mouse eat at home?
4. Why did the city mouse ask her friend to go to the city?
5. Why did the country mouse go back to the country?

Checkpoint 3

Read the sentences below. What do the underlined words stand for?

1. Seeds and plants were all the country mouse had to eat. So <u>she</u> gave seeds and plants to the city mouse to eat.
   a. the country mouse   b. the city mouse

2. The city mouse laughed. "We got away from the cat that time," <u>she</u> said.
   a. the cat   b. the city mouse

Interesting Pets and Friendly People

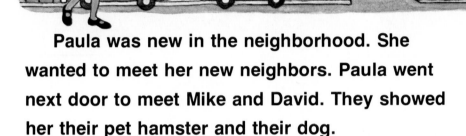

Paula was new in the neighborhood. She wanted to meet her new neighbors. Paula went next door to meet Mike and David. They showed her their pet hamster and their dog.

Mike and David took Paula to meet Nick and Nadine. They lived above their mother's grocery store. Paula met their turtle and their rabbit.

Paula liked her new neighborhood. There were lots of interesting pets and friendly people.

Think about skills

Do you ever sort socks? Do you ever sort dishes or toys? You often need to put things into groups because they all are the same color, shape, or size. Objects can be grouped together because they are alike in other ways too.

1. Why can these objects be grouped together?

2. Here are some of Paula's neighbors. Put them into two groups. Name the groups.

a. Mike   b.   c.   d. Nadine

e.   f. David   g. Nick   h.

Practice skills

1. Put these objects into two groups. Name one group Plants. Name the other Things to Read.

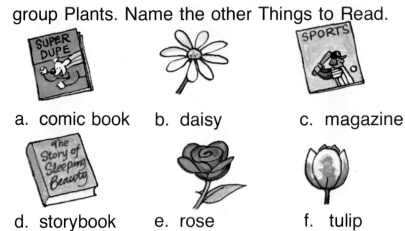

a. comic book   b. daisy   c. magazine

d. storybook   e. rose   f. tulip

THE TRAVELING ZOO

Today some of the animals from the zoo are going to a library. People at the library will be able to learn about a bird, a reptile, and a mammal.

A barn owl is going to the library. The owl is put into a special case for the trip.

A snake is going too. The snake will travel in a cloth bag.

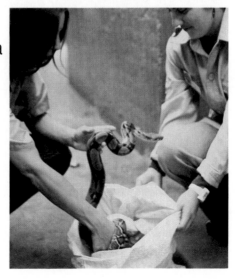

Do you know what animal
this is?
It is a kinkajou.
The kinkajou is going
to the library too.

The people who take the animals from the zoo are
trained to know all about the animals. They carefully
carry the animals into the library.

Do you know which animal is the bird? the reptile?
the mammal?

40

Out comes the kinkajou! The kinkajou is a mammal.
Mammals always have hair or fur on their bodies.

Kinkajous usually live in trees. They hold onto
branches with their long tails.

The woman tells the people about the kinkajou.
Everyone wants to touch the furry animal.

The snake is a boa constrictor. Snakes are reptiles. Reptiles have scales on their bodies.

The barn owl is a bird. Birds have feathers. Birds also have wings and most birds fly.

Do you see the glove the woman is wearing? The glove protects her hand from the owl's claws.

Barn owls usually sleep during the day. At night they hunt for food.

4: Apply

The people at the library asked questions about the animals. Some said they would visit these animals the next time they went to the zoo. After the show, the animals are taken back to their homes in the zoo.

On other days the animals shown below are part of the traveling zoo. The parrot is a bird. The turtle is a reptile. The ferret is a mammal.

Think about the selection

1. How does a kinkajou hold onto branches?
2. What do snakes have on their bodies?
3. When does a barn owl usually sleep?

Checkpoint 4

1. Which animals below are mammals?
2. Which animals below are birds?

a. kinkajou

b. parrot

c. owl

d. ferret

A CAT IS

by
Adrien
Stoutenburg

A cat is

always a kitten first,
which is mostly fluff
with a tail fastened on.
And four round legs
just long enough
to keep him up
instead of down.

A kitten is quiet
and full of sleep
except when he's awake
and mewing,
and climbing where
he shouldn't climb,
and doing things
he shouldn't be doing—

But kittens must do
the things they want to
if they want to be kittens
and grow into cats,
which, of course, they do.

Wouldn't you?

Bonus
Selection

5

Main idea

What Is the Main Idea?

A mother rabbit makes a nest. First she digs a small hole. Then she puts grass and bits of her fur in it. The nest will be soft.

Think about skills

Every story has a main idea. The main idea is what the story is all about. The story you read tells how a mother rabbit makes a nest. The main idea is: a mother rabbit makes a nest.

Judy ran outside. The sun was out, but it was raining. Soon Judy saw a rainbow. It was red, orange, yellow, blue, and green.

1. What is the main idea?
   a. It was raining.
   b. The sun was shining.
   c. Judy saw a rainbow.

46

Practice skills

Some people have dangerous jobs. Mario's mother has a dangerous job. She works high off the ground. She works on telephone wires.

1. What is the main idea?
   a. Some people have dangerous jobs.
   b. Mario's mother is busy.
   c. Telephone wires are high off the ground.

Winter will be here soon. The squirrel is looking for nuts to hide away. The squirrel will eat them when winter comes.

2. What is the main idea?
   a. The squirrel makes a nest.
   b. The squirrel gets ready for winter.
   c. The squirrel likes winter.

Find a Way

by Vivian Thompson

Once there was a wise woman. Other people would say, "I cannot do it. There is no way."

But the wise woman would say, "Think! Find a way."

One morning the wise woman said, "I'd like some fish to eat. I'll walk to the store and get some."

5: Apply

The wise woman got her basket and started out. On the way she saw a bent pin on the ground. She put it into her basket. "Who knows?" said the wise woman. "I may need a bent pin."

Next she came to a field. She saw six tin cans. She put the cans into her basket. "Who knows?" said the wise woman. "I may need six tin cans."

The wise woman went on.

Soon the wise woman met Miguel. "I want to fish," said Miguel. "But I have no hooks."

"Think! Find a way," said the wise woman.

She reached into her basket and brought out the bent pin.

"Can you find a way with this?" asked the wise woman.

"Oh, yes! I know a good way," said Miguel.

The wise woman went on.

50

Soon she met Jake, Kim, and Su Lin. "Why are you so sad?" asked the wise woman.

"We want to walk on stilts," said Kim.

"Think! Find a way," said the wise woman.

She reached into her basket and brought out the six tin cans.

"Can you find a way with these?" she asked.

"Oh, yes! I know a good way," said Kim.

The wise woman went on.

The wise woman reached the store. But there were no fish left.

"Oh, well," she said. "I had a good walk. I'll have fish another day."

5: *Apply*

The wise woman started home. Soon she met Jake,
Kim, and Su Lin.

"Look at us!" they said. "This is fun! Why don't you
take a turn?"

The wise woman tried the tin-can stilts. It was fun to
walk on them. She gave them back and went on.

Soon the wise woman met Miguel.

"Look at the fish I caught! These two are for you," said
Miguel.

"Thank you," said the wise woman. "I will have fish to
eat after all. I'll go home and cook them right now.
That will be fun too."

And it was.

54

Think about the selection

1. What did the wise woman give Miguel?

2. What did the wise woman give Jake, Kim, and Su Lin?

3. Which pictures show what happened first? next? last?

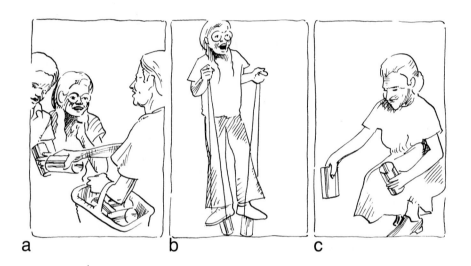

a   b   c

Checkpoint 5

1. What is the main idea of the story?

   a. A wise woman found some tin cans.

   b. A wise woman went to the store for some fish.

   c. A wise woman helped some children find a way to do something they wanted to do.

Linda Tests Her Bike

First Linda got her hat and coat. She put these things in her bike basket. Then she took the lock off her bike. She was going to the park to check her bike wheels.

Linda shut the gate and made a left turn. She rode five blocks to Rico's house. She wanted to see if he could go to the park.

Linda asked Rico's mama, "Can Rico go with me to North Park? I need to test my bike. My folks have a rule. I must check each wheel when I start riding my bike to school."

Rico said, "Please, may I go? I need to check my bike too."

"Yes," said his mama. "I will fix you some cheese sandwiches and milk. Then you can have lunch at the park."

Think about skills

➤➤ A vowel letter stands for more than one sound.
Two vowel letters together usually stand for
one sound. ◀◀

Words like *hat, check, if, blocks,* and *must* usually
have a short vowel sound.
Words like *park, her, first, north,* and *turn* usually
have an r-controlled vowel sound.
Words like *made, these, bike, rode, rule, each, please,
need,* and *cheese* usually have a long vowel sound.
Words like *me, go,* and *my* usually also have a long
vowel sound.

**Linda and Rico saw a cute chipmunk eat a nut.
Rico and Linda had their cheese sandwiches. Then
they checked the wheels on the bikes. They went
for a ride. But they did not go very far.**

then	ride	nut	did	go
cute	cheese	had	eat	far

1. Which words have short vowel sounds?
2. Which words have long vowel sounds?
3. Which word has an r-controlled vowel sound?

Practice skills

When Rico got home,
his brother Juan was
waiting for him.

Juan said, "Will you
read to me? I like
this book best. But
it's too hard for me."

"I don't have time
now," said Rico.
"Mama asked me to
stir the soup. I'll
read to you later.
You can curl up in my
lap and turn the page."

page	curl	lap	will
stir	my	home	time
read	best	but	me

1. Which words have short vowel sounds?
2. Which words have long vowel sounds?
3. Which words have r-controlled sounds?

THE LITTLE WHITE BOX

by Ruth Bishop Juline

Danny went skipping down the walk. In his hands was a little white box. He stopped at Felipe's house.

"Hello, Felipe," Danny called. "Guess what I have."

"A little white box," Felipe said.

"There's something in it," Danny said.

Adapted from "Joey's Little White Box" by Ruth Bishop Juline from *One Two*, February 11, 1973. Copyright © 1972 by Graded Press.

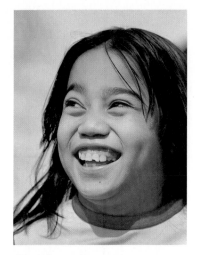

"A spinning top?" Carmen asked. She was
Felipe's sister.

"It rattles," Felipe said. "I think it's a stone."

"It isn't a spinning top or a stone,"
answered Danny.

Danny laughed. "You'll never guess so I'll tell you. I have some money in my little white box. I'm going to buy a candy bar, but I don't know what kind to buy."

"I would buy a peanut bar," Felipe said. "They're good."

"I would buy a chocolate bar," Carmen said.

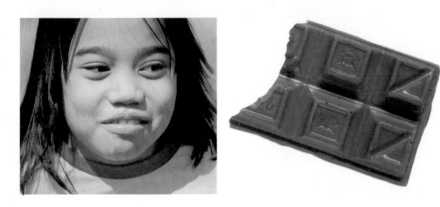

Danny hurried to the candy
shop. The clerk in the shop
asked, "What do you want?"

"I want a candy bar,"
Danny said. But all the
candy bars looked very small.

Danny thought about
Carmen and Felipe. Right
away he had an idea.

"I'll take jellybeans,"
said Danny.

Danny watched the
clerk fill a bag with
jellybeans. Danny took
the money from the
little white box
and handed it to the clerk.

Then he hurried back to Felipe's house.
Felipe and Carmen were in the
yard jumping rope.

"Guess what I have in this bag,"
Danny called to them.

"A candy bar!" the others cried.

"No," Danny said. "I have candy for
each of us."

Then they sat on the front porch and everyone ate some candy.

"This is better than eating a candy bar by myself," Danny said.

Carmen and Felipe thought so too!

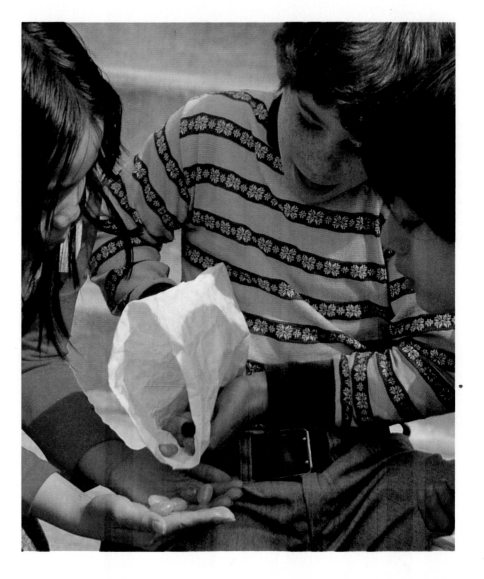

Think about the selection

1. What did Danny have?
2. What did Carmen think was in the box?
3. What did Felipe think was in the box?
4. What was in Danny's box?
5. What did Danny buy? Why?
6. Do you think Danny's idea was a good one? Why or why not?
7. What two words does each word below stand for?
   a. isn't   b. I'll   c. they're

Checkpoint 6

box	my	clerk	sat	stone	went
porch	bar	each	so	but	take

1. Which words have short vowel sounds?
2. Which words have long vowel sounds?
3. Which words have r-controlled vowel sounds?

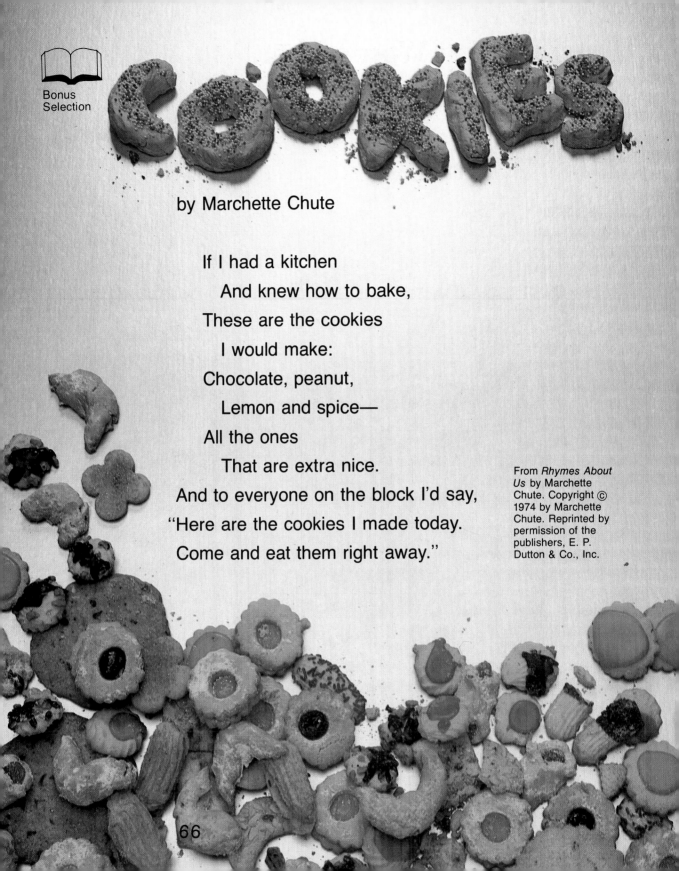

COOKIES

by Marchette Chute

If I had a kitchen
  And knew how to bake,
These are the cookies
  I would make:
Chocolate, peanut,
  Lemon and spice—
All the ones
  That are extra nice.
And to everyone on the block I'd say,
"Here are the cookies I made today.
Come and eat them right away."

Figuring Out Words That Fit

» If you see a word you don't know in a sentence,
try to think of one that makes sense. Then check to
see if the consonant sounds in your word match
the printed word. «

1. What words fit in the sentence below?

Roberto _____ lunch.

You may have thought of many words that fit.
Cooked, fixed, ate, enjoyed, and *missed* all fit.
You need more clues.

Roberto _____ lunch. Soon it was ready.

2. Now do you know which word fits? Either
cooked or *fixed* fit. Here are some more clues.

Roberto c____ lunch. Soon it was ready.

3. What word fits? If you said *cooked,* you were
right. The missing word starts with *c,* and *cooked*
makes sense in the story.

4. What word fits in the sentence below?
Roberto sat down at the t____ and began to eat.

Practice skills

Use the clues in each sentence to find the word
that fits.

1. Darla likes to ride in a sn___ .

snake   snowmobile   car

2. Barry is taking g___ lessons.

flute   goat   guitar

3. Koji put his socks in a dr___ .

drawer   box   dragon

4. Amy is eating a c___ .

peach   carrot   coat

WORKING TOGETHER

This is the Bourke family.
They sell puppets.
The Bourkes also put on
puppet shows for schools
and parties.

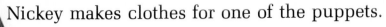

Nickey makes clothes for one of the puppets.

Mike and Brian make sure the strings of the puppets are all right.

Everyone helps get
ready for the show.
A sign is made to tell
people when the
show begins.

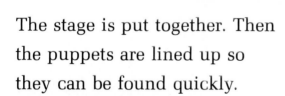

The stage is put together. Then
the puppets are lined up so
they can be found quickly.

Now the show begins!

7: Apply

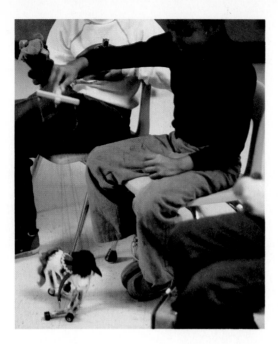

After the show, the Bourkes take the puppets into the audience. The children in the audience get to try the puppets. Some of the children think this is the most fun of all!

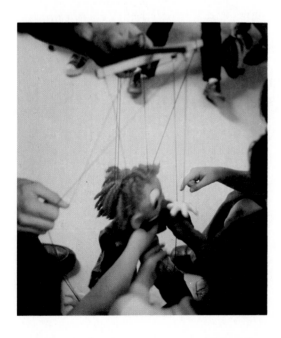

Think about the selection

1. What is the main idea of "Working Together"?

   a. Children in the audience get to try the puppets.
   b. The stage has to be put together.
   c. The Bourke family puts on puppet shows.

2. What happened first? next? last?

   a. The stage was put up.
   b. A puppet show was put on.
   c. The puppets were lined up.

Checkpoint 7

Which word fits the sentence?

1. Mike helped put on the p____ show.
   petal   puppet   dog

2. The boys made sure the str___ of the puppets were all right.
   heads   streets   strings

3. The Bourkes s____ puppets in their store.
   sell   make   some

7: Assess

HOW TO MAKE A PUPPET

You will need:

a sock

felt pen

cotton or crumpled paper

2 rubber bands

colored felt or paper

glue

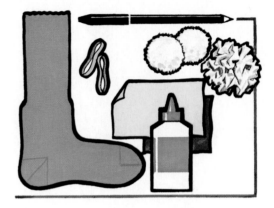

To make a puppet:

1. Put your hand in the sock. Your fingers should be in the toe of the sock. Your thumb should be in the heel. Open and close your hand.

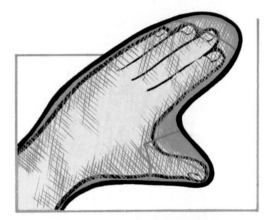

2. Use a felt pen to mark on the sock where you think the ears should be. Take your hand out of the sock.

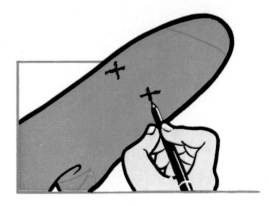

75

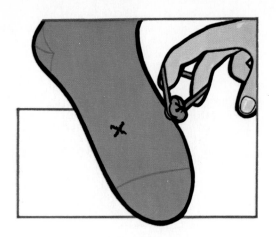

3. Find one of the pen marks.
   Pull up a little of the
   sock at the mark. Wrap
   a rubber band around it.
   Do the same thing at the
   other pen mark. Now
   your puppet has ears.

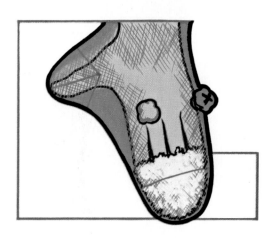

4. To make a nose, push
   cotton or crumpled paper
   into the toe of the sock.
   Make sure you can still
   put your fingers in the
   toe to open and close
   the puppet's mouth.

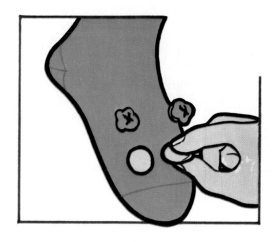

5. Cut eyes out
   of colored felt or paper.
   Glue them on the puppet
   where you want them.

Here are some other ideas you
might like to try. Sew yarn
on the puppet for hair.
Sew on buttons for eyes and
nose.

To make a snake puppet, do
not stuff the toe. Use pipe
cleaners for a tongue.

Think about the selection

1. What kind of puppet will you make? What will you
   need to make it?
2. How can you make ears on a sock puppet?

The Biggest Splash

The children wanted to find out who could make the biggest splash. John said he could. Bill thought he could because he was bigger than John. Sally was sure she could.

Sally shouted, "Go!" The children started to run. They went running to the pool. When they jumped in, they all hit the water at the same time. What a big splash! They hopped out of the pool, looked at each other, and laughed! No one had seen who made the biggest splash.

Then the children had to eat lunch. After they had eaten, they tried again. They still wanted to know who could make the biggest splash.

8: Teach

Think about skills

» Letters can be added at the end of words to make new words. The letters *en, ed, ing, er,* and *est* are endings. Words to which endings are added are root words. Sometimes a final consonant letter in a root word is doubled before an ending is added. «

You saw these words in the story.

eat   big   run

eaten   bigger   running

1. Which words are root words?
2. What ending do you see in *eaten?* in *bigger?* in *running?*

You saw these words too.

wanted   biggest   hopped

3. What endings do you see?
4. Which words have a final consonant letter doubled before an ending?

You read that Bill was bigger than John.

5. Which sentence below would tell about John?
   John was smaller than Bill.
   John was bigger than Bill.

Practice skills

Write the root word in each underlined word.

1. Bill <u>hopped</u> from the pool.
2. He <u>landed</u> on the grass.

3. Sally was <u>winning</u> the race.
4. She was <u>running</u> fast.

5. John <u>splashed</u> in the pool.
6. His splash was the <u>highest</u>.

7. Sally had <u>beaten</u> John.
8. She ran the <u>fastest</u>.

Look at the picture. Then answer the questions below.

 9. Is Sally bigger than John?
10. Is Sally smaller than John?

THE BIG ENORMOUS CARROT

By Dorothy Gordon

Vicki had a garden. She worked hard in her garden. She had lettuce and radishes. She had other things too. But the best things in her garden were her carrots. Her carrots were big and fat and orange.

One carrot was enormous. "It is the biggest carrot in the world," said Vicki. "I will take it to the fair. It will be the best carrot at the fair."

Vicki pulled her big enormous carrot. She washed
it carefully. She laid it on the grass to dry. Then
she went into the house to get a sack.

That day Wiggly, Mr. Jones's big rabbit, got out of
his cage again. He hopped into Vicki's garden. He
saw the big enormous carrot on the grass. He
began to eat it. It was good.

Vicki came out of the house with her sack. She saw Wiggly eating her carrot. "Go away, you awful rabbit," she yelled. "Get out of my garden!"

Wiggly kept right on eating the big enormous carrot.

"Get out of here!" Vicki shouted again.

Mr. Jones came running. "Wiggly got out of his cage again," he said. "What has he done?"

"He has eaten my big enormous carrot. Now I can't take it to the fair," Vicki said.

"That's pretty bad," said Mr. Jones. "What can we do about it?"

"We can't do anything about it," answered Vicki.

Wiggly had just finished off the carrot. He sat there wiggling his nose and looking very happy.

Mr. Jones thought for a while. Then he said, "Your carrot can go to the fair."

"How can my carrot go to the fair?" Vicki asked. "It is inside of Wiggly."

"I will give Wiggly to you," Mr. Jones answered. "He is your rabbit now. You can take Wiggly to the fair. He is a good rabbit. He will win a prize for you."

So Vicki took Wiggly to the fair. He was the best rabbit there. Vicki got a blue ribbon and a trophy. On the top of the trophy was a little bronze rabbit. The rabbit was eating a carrot.

So Vicki's big enormous carrot went to the fair after all.

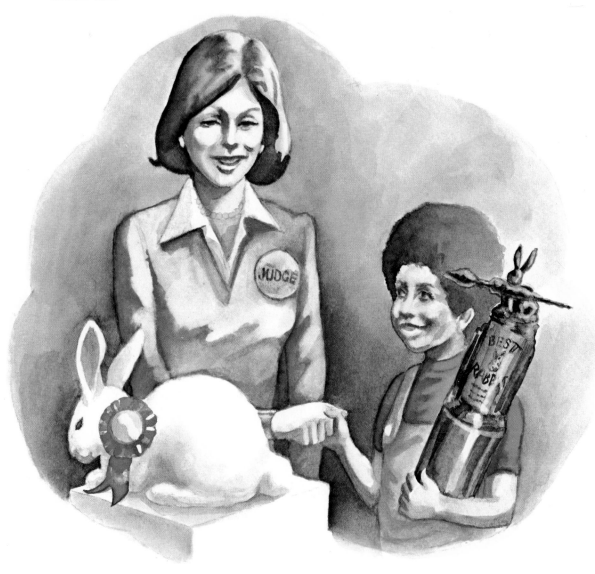

Think about the selection

1. Find something Vicki said in the story. Read it aloud the way you think she said it.
2. What did Vicki get at the fair?
3. Which pictures show what happened first? next? last?

a

b

c

Checkpoint 8

1. What is the root word and ending in each word below?

   eaten   shouted   hopped
   biggest   running   washed

2. Which is the smallest?

   a. lettuce   b. radish   c. carrot

cookies Arnie baked us for

Scrambled Sentences

The children hurried into their room. They saw
a strange sentence on the board.

"What does it mean?" asked Kiku and Carlos.

Mr. Johnson said, "This is a scrambled sentence.
The words make sense if they are put in
alphabetical order."

"I see words starting with *a, b,* and *c.* But there's
no word starting with *d,*" said Mark.

"Then look for a word that starts with the next
letter of the alphabet. Keep going until you've
gone all the way through the alphabet,"
Mr. Johnson said.

"I know!" Julie said. "Arnie baked cookies for us."

"Very good," said Mr. Johnson. **"Now sit in alphabetical order. Arnie will hand out the cookies."**

Think about skills

1. Below are the names of the children in Mr. Johnson's class. Put the names in alphabetical order.

Pablo	Wanda	Kiku
Bess	Carlos	Julie
Theresa	Mark	David

Practice skills

Here are more scrambled sentences. Put the words in alphabetical order.

1. quickly finished jobs her Cora
2. is birthday today Anne's
3. Edgar his frightened rabbit pet
4. food well always very chew
5. joined Donna team our swimming
6. window hopped a the giant in
7. tricks do silly of lots clowns
8. squirrels Bob gray eight counted

LET'S WALK UP A WALL

by Ryerson Johnson

There are some things that animals can do that
people can't do.

Can you walk up a wall?
A centipede can walk up a wall.

9: Apply

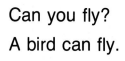

Can you fly?
A bird can fly.

Can you pick
a leaf from high
in a tree?
A giraffe can
pick a leaf from
high in a tree.

But there are many things that people can do that
animals can't do.

Can an animal
use scissors?

Can an animal
read a book?

Can an animal
write a letter?

People can do so many things animals can't do
because PEOPLE CAN THINK!

People can even do many of the special things that animals can do. That's because people can think of ways to do them.

Do you want to
fly like a bird?
You can if you
use an airplane.

Do you want to
pick a leaf from
high in a tree?
You can if you
use a ladder.

92

People are always thinking of new ways to do things—and then doing them. You might be the person who thinks of a way to walk up a wall.

Think about the selection

1. What is the main idea of "Let's Walk Up a Wall?"
2. In which word do you hear the m sound at the beginning? in the middle? at the end?

   many   from   animals
3. Which words begin with two consonant sounds?

   to   tree   fly   leaf
4. Which words begin like *third?*

   thing   high   top   think
5. Which words begin with the same sound as *city?*

   can   so   centipede
6. In which words do you hear the k sound?

   pick   city   because   book

Checkpoint 9

1. What letters are missing from the alphabet below?

   a _ c d _ _ g _ i _ _ l m _ o p _
   r s _ u v _ _ y _
2. Put these words from the story in alphabetical order.

leaf	think	airplane
people	bird	scissors
centipede	wall	giraffe

JUST AS I DO

by Ethel and Leonard Kessler

Abridged from *Do Baby Bears Sit in Chairs?* by Ethel and Leonard Kessler. Copyright © 1961 by Ethel and Leonard Kessler. Used by permission of Doubleday & Company, Inc.

Do ladybugs
drink from mugs,
roll on rugs,
give great big hugs?

Oh no!
But they can creep, creep, creep,
just as I do.

Do little chicks
pick up sticks,
build with bricks,
play funny tricks?

No, no, no.
But they munch on corn,
just as I do.

95

Section One Checkpoint

Word Identification Tests

Subtest 1

1.	ⓐ shook	ⓑ look	ⓒ book	ⓓ DK
2.	ⓐ candy	ⓑ carry	ⓒ city	ⓓ DK
3.	ⓐ guitar	ⓑ giant	ⓒ paint	ⓓ DK
4.	ⓐ hamper	ⓑ hamster	ⓒ hammer	ⓓ DK

stop

Subtest 2

5. long	ⓐ shed	ⓑ she	ⓒ spell	ⓓ DK
6. short	ⓐ hurt	ⓑ hug	ⓒ huge	ⓓ DK
7. long	ⓐ fin	ⓑ first	ⓒ fine	ⓓ DK
8. r-controlled	ⓐ curl	ⓑ pride	ⓒ cart	ⓓ DK
9. long	ⓐ not	ⓑ for	ⓒ so	ⓓ DK

stop

Subtest 3

ⓐ people ⓑ floor	14. ⓐ around ⓑ parade
ⓒ bigger ⓓ DK	ⓒ asked ⓓ DK
10. ⓐ lunches ⓑ cookie	15. ⓐ reddest ⓑ best
ⓒ because ⓓ DK	ⓒ wash ⓓ DK
11. ⓐ animal ⓑ begins	16. ⓐ stand ⓑ eaten
ⓒ believe ⓓ DK	ⓒ alike ⓓ DK
12. ⓐ worked ⓑ place	17. ⓐ branch ⓑ fanning
ⓒ kinkajou ⓓ DK	ⓒ little ⓓ DK
13. ⓐ hopping ⓑ heavy	18. ⓐ began ⓑ winter
ⓒ button ⓓ DK	ⓒ helper ⓓ DK

stop

Subtest 4

19. Mari climbs a l____ .

     ⓐ lemon   ⓑ ladder   ⓒ tree   ⓓ DK

20. Carlos plays a fl____ .

     ⓐ drum   ⓑ fly   ⓒ flute   ⓓ DK

21. Danny likes to eat a p____ .

     ⓐ peach   ⓑ park   ⓒ raisin   ⓓ DK

22. Sally's skirt is gr____ .

     ⓐ blue   ⓑ green   ⓒ ground   ⓓ DK

stop

Subtest 5

23. ⓐ again	ⓑ away	
ⓒ across	ⓓ DK	

24. ⓐ their	ⓑ than	
ⓒ today	ⓓ DK	

25. ⓐ once	ⓑ old	
ⓒ order	ⓓ DK	

26. ⓐ before	ⓑ began	
ⓒ because	ⓓ DK	

27. ⓐ guess ⓑ gate
    ⓒ give ⓓ DK

28. ⓐ store ⓑ start
    ⓒ sure ⓓ DK

29. ⓐ thought ⓑ touch
    ⓒ through ⓓ DK

30. ⓐ well ⓑ wise
    ⓒ while ⓓ DK

Possible Word Identification Score: 30   **stop**

Comprehension Tests

Subtest 6

Which is smallest?

ⓐ   ⓑ   ⓒ   ⓓ DK

1. Which is bigger?

ⓐ   ⓑ   ⓒ DK

2. Which is longest?

ⓐ   ⓑ   ⓒ   ⓓ DK

stop

98

Some animals can change their color. They change to match the color of a green leaf or a brown twig. Then their enemies can't see them very well.

3. What is the main idea?
   ⓐ Some animals can change their color.
   ⓑ Some animals can be green or brown.
   ⓒ Some animals have enemies.
   ⓓ DK

Some cats have long tails. Some have short ones. Some cats have long hair. Some have short hair. Some cats are very big. Some are small. Some have stripes. Some have spots. Some cats make good pets. Lions and tigers are cats. They don't make good pets.

4. What is the main idea?
   ⓐ Some cats have stripes.
   ⓑ Lions don't make good pets.
   ⓒ There are many kinds of cats.
   ⓓ DK

stop

Subtest 8

	ⓐ	ⓑ	ⓒ	ⓓ	ⓔ DK
5.	ⓐ	ⓑ	ⓒ	ⓓ	ⓔ DK
6.	ⓐ	ⓑ	ⓒ	ⓓ	ⓔ DK
7.	ⓐ	ⓑ	ⓒ	ⓓ	ⓔ DK

Possible Comprehension Score: 7 **stop**

Study and Research Test

Subtest 9

	ⓐ Carmen	ⓑ Judy	ⓒ Mike	ⓓ Brian	ⓔ DK
1.	ⓐ job	ⓑ feet	ⓒ horn	ⓓ garden	ⓔ DK
2.	ⓐ order	ⓑ its	ⓒ else	ⓓ along	ⓔ DK
3.	ⓐ Kiku	ⓑ Rico	ⓒ Paula	ⓓ Tomi	ⓔ DK
4.	ⓐ sat	ⓑ us	ⓒ yes	ⓓ winter	ⓔ DK

Possible Study and Research Score: 4 **stop**

THE BOY AND HIS GOATS
A Scandinavian Folk Tale

Gold Medal
Selection

Once upon a time a boy had three goats.

Every day the boy took the goats up a green hill
to eat grass.

One day the boy went to sleep while the goats
were eating grass.

Then the goats got in the garden.

The boy woke up and saw the goats in the garden.

He chased the goats. But he couldn't get them out of the garden.

The boy sat down and began to cry. Soon a rabbit came along. The rabbit said, "Why are you crying?"

The boy said, "I'm crying because I can't get the goats out of the garden."

The rabbit said, "Don't cry. I can get them out of the garden."

The rabbit chased the goats. But he couldn't get them out of the garden.

The rabbit sat down and began to cry.

Soon a fox came along. The fox said, "Why are you crying?"

The rabbit said, "I'm crying because the boy is crying. The boy is crying because he can't get the goats out of the garden."

The fox said, "Don't cry. I can get them out of the garden."

The fox chased the goats. But she couldn't get them out of the garden.

The fox sat down and began to cry.

Soon a wolf came along. The wolf said, "Why are you crying?"

The fox said, "I'm crying because the rabbit is crying. The rabbit is crying because the boy is crying. The boy is crying because he can't get the goats out of the garden."

The wolf said, "Don't cry. I can get them out of the garden."

The wolf chased the goats. But he couldn't get them out of the garden.

The wolf sat down and began to cry.

Soon a bee came along. The bee said, "Why are you crying?"

The wolf said, "I'm crying because the fox is crying. The fox is crying because the rabbit is crying. The rabbit is crying because the boy is crying. The boy is crying because he can't get the goats out of the garden."

The bee said, "Don't cry. I can get them out of the garden."

The boy said, "How can you do what a boy, a rabbit, a fox, and a wolf can't do?"

The bee said, "I'll show you."

The bee went after the goats. BUZZ! BUZZ! BUZZ! BUZZ! BUZZ! BUZZ!

The goats didn't want the bee to sting them. So they ran out of the garden.

And that's how a little bee could do what a boy, a rabbit, a fox, and a wolf couldn't do.

Section Two

What's a Mongoose?

Do you know what a mongoose is? If you don't, you can find out by looking in a dictionary or a glossary.

Page 113 shows part of a glossary. The first entry word is **mongoose.**

An *entry word* is a word that is explained. It is printed in very dark type. An *entry* is an entry word and everything that goes with it.

The entry for **mongoose** has three parts. They are the entry word, the definition, and the picture.

One or more definitions come right after the entry word. A *definition* tells you what a word means.

Some entries have a *picture* to help explain one of the definitions of the entry word.

Guide words are at the top of the page. *Guide words* tell the first and last entries on a page. All entry words on a dictionary or glossary page are in alphabetical order.

10: Teach

entry word   entry   definition   picture   guide words

mongoose

owl

M   m

mon goose a very long, thin animal that kills snakes. See the picture.

muf fler 1. a warm scarf worn around one's neck.
2. part of a car that takes away noise.

mongoose

N   n

nail 1. a small, pointed piece of metal that can be hammered into wood. See the picture.
2. the hard part on top of the end of a finger or toe.

nap a short sleep.

nod let your head fall forward when you are sleepy or falling asleep.

nail   1.

O   o

ov en a space in a stove for baking food.

owl a bird with big eyes and a short, curved bill. See the picture.

owl

Find pages 230 and 231 in the Glossary.

1. What are the guide words on page 231?
2. Could the word *dust* be on this page? Why or why not?
3. What is the definition of the entry word **glide?**
4. Which definition of the entry word **entry** is shown in the picture?

Practice skills

Find page 236 in the Glossary.

1. What are the guide words on page 236?
2. Could the word *trade* be on this page? Why or why not?
3. What is the definition of the entry word **trophy?**
4. Which definition of the entry word **train** is shown in the picture?

SERENDIPITY

by Eve Rice

Willie Brimble was wondering if there might be a piece of cake left. Just then his sister Polly walked by.

"Serendipity," Willie said.

"What's that?" asked Polly.

"A word," Willie answered. "I like the sound, but I don't know what it means."

"Let's look it up in a dictionary," Polly said.

10: Apply

Polly and Willie went to the bookcase.

"The dictionary is gone!" Willie said.

"Yes, but look," said Polly. "Here is my skate key. I have been looking for it."

"That won't help us find what *serendipity* means," said Willie. "Come on."

Polly put the skate key in her pocket.

116

They went to the desk.
There were many books
on the desk, but the
dictionary was not there.

"Oh," said Polly.
"My bookmark! I've been
looking for it."

Just then the door slammed. "Hello," called Mrs. Brimble.

Polly and Willie ran to the door. "Do you know where the dictionary is?" they asked.

"I think it's on the kitchen table," said Mrs. Brimble. She was right. The dictionary was there.

Polly stopped by the sink.
"Here is my jar of blue
paint. I lost it this morning.
I'm glad I found it," Polly
said. "Now let's find our
word."

They turned the pages of the dictionary. Finally they came to *serendipity.*

Polly laughed. Then she said, "Serendipity means being able to discover good things by accident.

"Well, I discovered my skate key, my bookmark, and my blue paint today—all by accident."

"Yes," Willie said. "And we found a good word too."

10: Apply

Think about the selection

1. What two root words do you see in *bookmark?*

2. What three things did Polly discover by accident?

3. Why did Polly and Willie want to find a dictionary?

Checkpoint 10 ▬▬▬▬▬▬▬

Find page 235 in the Glossary.

1. What are the guide words on this page?

2. Find the entry for **sink.** What are its definitions?

3. What else beside the definition helps you know what a sink is?

4. Could an entry for **accident** be on this page?

5. Polly found her paint beside the sink.
   Which definition of **sink** fits this sentence?

Tad's Return

Tad had been on vacation. Tad's friends did not know he was home. Tad felt lonely.

Tad called his friends. All of them came over to his house. They were happy to see Tad and hear about his trip.

Think about skills

Some stories tell you how a person feels about someone or something. You know Tad felt lonely at the beginning of the story because the story tells you this.

Sometimes you have to guess how someone in the story feels. You can do this by thinking about what that person does in the story. You can also think about how you would feel if you were that person.

11: Teach

1. How did Tad's friends feel about him?

If you said they liked him, you were right. You can tell this is so because Tad's friends were happy he was home again.

2. How do you think Tad felt at the end of the story? What makes you think as you do?

Practice skills

Barb was excited because it was time for cartoons. She ran into the living room to turn on the TV.

Barb's sister Pam was watching a football game. "Do you want to watch the game with me?" Pam asked.

"No," mumbled Barb as she left the room.

1. How did Barb feel about watching cartoons?
2. What was Pam watching on TV?
3. How do you think Barb felt when she saw what Pam was watching? What makes you think as you do?

Two Good Friends

by Judy Delton

Duck had cleaned his house. He was looking at his nice clean rooms. Then he heard a knock at the door. It was Bear. "Come in," said Duck. "But wipe your feet."

Taken from *Two Good Friends* by Judy Delton. Text © 1974 by Judy Delton. Used by permission of Crown Publishers, Inc.

Bear wiped his feet. Then he went inside and sat down. He put his feet on Duck's table. Duck reached for a paper. He put it under Bear's feet.

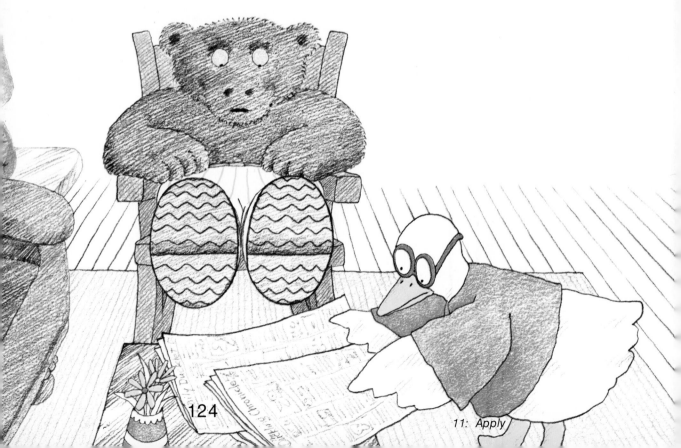

124

"What do you have to eat?" asked Bear.

"Nothing," said Duck. "Today I cleaned my house. I did not bake."

"I have something," said Bear. He reached into his pocket and took out two little cakes.

"Bear," said Duck. "You are spilling crumbs on my floor." He reached for another paper. Then he put it under Bear's chair.

"Duck," Bear said. "You are a very good housekeeper. But what good is a clean house if you have nothing to eat? Have a cake."

Bear and Duck each ate a cake. They spent the rest of the afternoon doing a puzzle.

The next day Duck went to visit Bear.

"What smells so good?" asked Duck.

"I've been baking," said Bear. He pointed to
a honey cake and an apple pie on the table.
"Brush the flour off a chair and sit down."

"Bear," said Duck. "I can't sit down. My feet are
stuck."

11: Apply

"Oh dear," said Bear. "That's the honey. Would you like honey cake or apple pie?"

"Apple pie," said Duck. He had finally gotten his feet unstuck. "I've had enough honey for one day."

"OK," said Bear. He cut one piece of apple pie for Duck and one for himself.

"May I have a plate?" asked Duck.

"The plates are dirty," said Bear.

"Then may I have a fork?" asked Duck.

"The forks are dirty too," said Bear.

"Bear," said Duck. "How can I eat this pie?"

"I'm sorry," said Bear. "Today I baked. I didn't
clean the house or wash the dishes. Maybe you
can use your wings. The pie will still taste good."

When Duck finished, he licked the tips of his
wings. "I must say, Bear, you are a terrible
housekeeper. But your apple pie is the best I have
ever tasted."

The next day Bear went to Duck's house with a surprise. Duck was not at home but Bear went inside anyway.

He put six little cakes on the table. Then he wrote a note. "From Bear," it said. After that, he went home.

When Bear walked into his house, he was surprised. "I must be in the wrong house," he thought. His feet did not stick to the floor. The dishes were washed.

Then he saw a note: "From Duck."

"I must thank Duck," thought Bear.

Just then there was a knock on the door. It was Duck.

"Thank you for the cakes," said Duck. "I was so surprised. And it's not even my birthday."

"And I have never seen my house so clean," said Bear. "I was surprised too."

"We really are good friends," said Duck.

"Yes!" cried Bear. "Now come in and have some cookies. But first, wipe your feet."

Think about the selection

1. What does the word *it* stand for in each sentence below?

   Then Bear wrote a note. "From Bear," *it* said.
   a. Duck   b. the note   c. the pencil

   Duck reached for a paper. He put *it* under Bear's feet.
   d. the feet   e. Duck   f. the paper

2. What happened first? next? last?
   a. Duck cleaned Bear's house.
   b. Duck cleaned his own house.
   c. Duck's feet got stuck in honey.

Checkpoint 11

1. What did Duck think smelled so good?

2. Who was a good housekeeper?

3. Who was a good cook?

4. How did Duck feel when he found the cakes?

5. Why were Duck and Bear such good friends?

Why?

Look at the cartoon below. Read what the boy is
saying in the first two pictures.

1. What is happening in the pictures?
2. Why is the bird holding an umbrella over the
    dog's foot?

Many things in a story happen for a reason. When you
are reading to find out why something happened,
you may see the words *because* or *since.* These
words sometimes tell you that you are going
to read why something happened.

**Mr. Ray gave Lisa a plant. Lisa went
to the library to get a book about
plants because she wanted
to know how to take care of
her new plant.**

3. Why did Lisa get a book about plants?

Practice skills

Martha and Benny went for a swim because it was a hot day. After their swim they felt cooler.

1. Why did Martha and Benny go for a swim?

Mr. Sanchez got his pole. Then he walked to the pond. Since it was a holiday, he could fish all day.

2. Why was Mr. Sanchez able to fish all day?

Gwen went to the store. She bought some peanut butter and bread. When she got home, Gwen found out that she had forgotten to buy some milk. So she went back to the store.

3. Why did Gwen go back to the store?

134

A BUS RIDE

These children go to school in Fort Worth, Texas. They are going to take a bus ride. On their trip they will learn how to ride a bus safely. First they wait at the bus stop for the bus to arrive.

The girls and boys learn where they pay to ride a bus. They drop their money into a large box.

The driver shows everyone the bus schedules. Bus schedules tell what time the bus leaves a stop.

The teacher points out the back door. The children will use this door to get off the bus so that other people can use the front door to get on the bus.

At the end of the trip, the boys and girls visit a park. They see a statue of a famous American cowboy named Will Rogers. He wrote lots of funny stories because he liked to make people laugh.

12: Apply

Think about the selection

1. What were the children going to learn on their bus trip?

2. What happened first? next? last?
   a. The children visited a park.
   b. The children waited at the bus stop.
   c. The children got off the bus.

3. Which of these words is the opposite of *stop?* of *front?* of *out?*
   a. back   b. in   c. go

Checkpoint 12

1. Why might the children need bus schedules?

2. Why did the children get off the bus using the back door?

3. Why did Will Rogers write funny stories?

The New Puppies

Mrs. Gomez showed Jan the new puppies. The littlest puppy was brown. Jan wanted to take it out of the box and pet it.

"The puppies are only a week old," Mrs. Gomez said with a smile. "They can't see or walk. They are too little to be petted."

Every week Jan hurried to see the puppies. At last the puppies could walk. They had their eyes open. Now Jan could pet them.

Mrs. Gomez had taken one puppy out of the box. She was smiling as she handed it to Jan. "This brown puppy got fatter," Mrs. Gomez said. "It is the fattest puppy now."

13: Teach

Think about skills

» The letters *s, es, ing, ed, en, er,* and *est* are endings.
Words to which endings are added are root words.
Sometimes a change is made in a root word before
an ending is added.
—The final consonant may be doubled.
—The final *e* may be dropped.
—The final *y* may be changed to *i*. «

You saw these words in the story.

pet	smile	puppy
petted	smiling	puppies

1. Which words are root words?
2. What endings do you see?
3. What changes were made in the root words?

You saw these words too.

littlest   hurried   taken   fatter

4. What endings do you see?
5. In which word was the final consonant doubled
   before an ending?
6. In which words was the final *e* dropped before
   an ending?
7. In which word was the final *y* changed to *i*
   before an ending?

Practice skills

The brown puppy wiggled in Jan's arms. It was biting Jan's finger and wagging its tail at the same time.

Jan carried the puppy back to the box. The puppy cried when she put it down.

"I think this puppy likes me," Jan said. "May I have it when it gets bigger?"

Mrs. Gomez nodded. "Run home and ask your parents," she said.

"This is the happiest day of my life!" Jan said as she skipped out the door.

You saw these words in the story.

wiggled	biting	wagging
carried	cried	bigger
nodded	happiest	skipped

1. What endings do you see?
2. What are the root words?

Possum Was Fooled

by Shirley Patterson

Possum hung by his tail from a branch of a tree.
He couldn't sleep so he stared at the ground.

Possum thought he saw his friend Snake.
Snake seemed to be bent across a stick.

"Are you asleep, Snake?" asked Possum.

There was no answer.

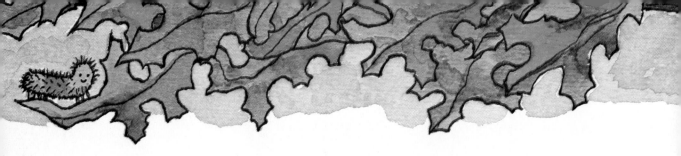

"Get up, or you'll hurt your back. You are bent in the middle," Possum said.

Snake still did not answer.

Possum was worried. He called to Raccoon.

Raccoon popped her head out of the tree trunk.

"Snake is bent," Possum said.

Raccoon leaned out of her nest to look. "You may be right," she said.

Soon Woodpecker hopped out of his hole in the tree. He wanted to see what was happening.

"Snake is bent," Possum said.

"You may be right," Woodpecker said.

The three friends decided
they must do something
to help Snake.

Possum said, "Perhaps
we can straighten Snake
by hanging him from a
tree. I find that very
comfortable."

"No," said Raccoon and
Woodpecker. "Snake
should *not* hang from
trees."

Then Woodpecker said,
"I could straighten Snake
with a few light taps
from my bill."

"No," Possum and
Raccoon said. "Your bill
is much too sharp."

Raccoon said, "Let's
move Snake off the
stick."

The three friends heard
Snake calling to them.

"What are you so excited about?" asked Snake.

Possum and Raccoon and Woodpecker saw Snake moving across the grass under the tree.

"There are two of him!" Raccoon cried.

"It was a trick!" Woodpecker said.

Snake laughed. "Did you think I was caught on that stick? That is my old skin."

148

Snake explained that sometimes he shed his old skin after he had grown a new one under it.

Raccoon and Woodpecker said, "Well, I never!"

Possum said, "I certainly was fooled!" Then he went to sleep.

Think about the selection

1. What is the main idea of the story?
   a. Woodpecker tapped Snake with his bill.
   b. Three animals were fooled because Snake shed his skin.
   c. Possum couldn't sleep so he talked to Woodpecker and Raccoon.
2. Why did Possum want to hang Snake from a tree?
3. Why did Snake shed his skin?

Checkpoint 13

You saw these words in the story.

straighten   popped   taps

moving   worried   happening

cried   decided   hopped

1. What endings do you see?
2. What are the root words?
3. In which words was the final consonant doubled before an ending?
4. In which words was the final e dropped before an ending?
5. In which words was the final y changed to i before an ending?
6. Which words had no spelling change before the ending?

150

Real or Make-Believe?

Bruce Takes a Walk

    Bruce went for a walk. He stopped when he saw a toy flute in a window. He wanted to buy it.

Gerri Flies to Town

    One day Gerri Giraffe said, "I will go to the store."

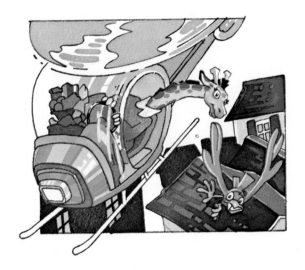

    Gerri flew her helicopter to town. She bought some fruit. Then she flew home.

Think about skills

    Which of these two stories could really have happened? You were right if you said "Bruce Takes a Walk." A person can really take a walk and see something in a window.

1. Could "Gerri Flies to Town" have happened?
2. Why do you think as you do?

14: Teach

Stories like "Gerri Flies to Town" are called make-believe because they could not really happen.

In make-believe stories you will often read about animals that talk, dress, and act like people.

A Picnic

Mr. Reed took Kay and Ricky to the park for a picnic. They went for a swim in the lake. Then they ate lunch.

3. Is the story above real or make-believe?
4. Why do you think as you do?

Practice skills

Mr. Fox ate his food too fast. He got very sick. He called Dr. Moose. She gave him some medicine.

1. Is the story above real or make-believe?
2. Why do you think as you do?

152

Gustav Green

by Ann Devendorf

Once upon a time, there lived a grasshopper by the
name of Gustav Green.

"Hop!" said his cousin Jumping Jack.

"Hop!" said his cousin Leaping Lena.

Gustav tried to hop. He could not.

"Like this," said Leaping Lena. And she hopped three
feet, six inches.

"Like this," said Jumping Jack. And he hopped three
feet, six inches.

"I can't get myself off the ground," said Gustav.

"Yes, you can," said Jumping Jack. "All grasshoppers hop."

"I can't," said Gustav. "I will have to walk through life—step, step, step!"

"Let's walk up to the top of this pile of hay," said Leaping Lena. "Then we'll hop off—one, two, three."

"All right," said Gustav.

The three grasshoppers walked up to the top of the pile of hay. Leaping Lena took a fine leap off the hay. Jumping Jack took a big jump off the hay. Gustav tried with all his might, but he just tumbled horns over heels off the pile of hay.

"Are you all right?" asked Leaping Lena.

"Yes," said Gustav. "But I am not going to try *that* again!"

"Let's try something else," said Leaping Lena.

"Yes," said Jumping Jack. "I will boost your left side. Leaping Lena will boost your right side. Then you will hop."

"All right," said Gustav.

14: Apply

Leaping Lena boosted. Jumping Jack boosted. Gustav stretched and stretched. He raised his head higher and higher and higher. He lost his balance. PLOP! The three grasshoppers tumbled down in a pile!

"It's no use," cried Gustav. "I'll be a walker."

"No, no!" said Jumping Jack. "Try again."

Gustav tried. He got his right jumping foot off the ground.

"Get your left jumping foot off the ground too," said Jumping Jack.

Gustav got his left foot off the ground but his right foot came down. Gustav gave a little hop on his right foot. His left foot came down. He gave a little hop on his left foot. His right foot came down. He gave a little hop.

"I'm skipping! I'm skipping!" called Gustav. "Look at me! Look at me!"

Gustav skipped around and around.

"A skipping grasshopper!" said Jumping Jack. "I've never seen a skipping grasshopper."

"Call me a grass-skipper," said Gustav with a smile.

158

"Yes," said Leaping Lena. "That's what you are—a grass-skipper. And do you know what?"

"What?" asked Gustav.

"It's nice to have a grass-skipper in the family," said Lena. "It's nice to have someone different around."

"Yes," said Jumping Jack. "It is."

Gustav grinned in happiness and skipped across the grass.

Think about the selection

1. Why did Leaping Lena and Jumping Jack want Gustav to hop?

2. Why did the three grasshoppers walk to the top of a pile of hay?

3. What two words does each word below stand for?
   that's   I'm   we'll

4. Read the first two paragraphs on page 154. Who did the word <u>you</u> stand for when Jumping Jack said "Yes, you can"?
   Gustav Green   Leaping Lena

5. Find something Gustav Green said in the story. Read it aloud the way you think he said it.

Checkpoint 14

1. Do you think the story "Gustav Green" is real or make-believe?

2. Why do you think as you do?

Ridiculous Riddles

» A vowel letter stands for more than one sound.
Two vowel letters together usually stand for
one sound. «

The words below have r-controlled, short, and long
vowel sounds.

a.	park	b.	cat	c.	gate	keep	me
	her		yes		these	cheese	go
	girl		big		five	clean	by
	horn		got		rope	please	
	turn		just		cute		

Use what you know about vowels to answer
the riddles.

1. It's something to eat.
   Its name has an r-controlled
   sound of *o*. What is it?

   corn   cone

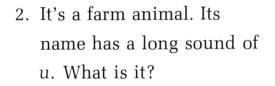

2. It's a farm animal. Its
   name has a long sound of
   u. What is it?

   duck   mule

3. It can grow. Its name
has a short sound of *a*.
What is it?

snake

plant

4. It's something cowboys
have. Its name has an
r-controlled sound of *u*.
What is it?

truck

spurs

5. It's a color. Its name
has a long sound of *e*.
What is it?

red

green

6. It's something that
can walk up a wall.
It's name has a long
sound of *i*. What is it?

bird

fly

In which words below do you hear short vowel
sounds? long vowel sounds? r-controlled vowel
sounds?

cone   snake   duck   truck   red   bird

162

Practice skills

1. It's a place where cows live. Its name has an r-controlled sound of *a*. What is it?

ranch   barn

2. It's something a baby wears. Its name has a short sound of *i*. What is it?

bib   shirt

3. It's something very hard. Its name has a short sound of *o*. What is it?

rock   bone

In which words below do you hear short vowel sounds? long vowel sounds? r-controlled vowel sounds?

ranch   shirt   bone

THE LITTLE PARK

by Dale Fife

Peter, Jill, and Ben saw the new sign.

"But this is where we play," said Peter. "It's not empty. Little things live here."

"I see a rabbit," Jill said.

"Look at the bees around the flowers," said Ben.

The children saw a grasshopper. A raccoon ran to its hiding place. A bird flew to its nest.

"Bugs and ants live in this log," Jill said. "People don't know. They say this land is empty."

Peter, Jill, and Ben looked around. What could they do?

Peter said, "We can make signs to tell people the land is not empty. I have a pencil."

"I have paper," Ben said.

"We can each make a sign," Jill said.

People came to see the empty ground for sale.
They were surprised to see the signs.

"It's like the woods here," a man said.

A woman said, "We have big buildings. But we
have no open space."

A police officer said, "There's no place for boys
and girls to play."

The people looked at each other. "We can ask the
mayor to keep this land for a park," they said.

And so the people went to the mayor.

He said, "I'll see what can be done."

In time the mayor said, "We'll do what the people
want. We'll use this land for a park."

"Now we have a place to play," said Jill.

"And the animals have a place to live,"
said Ben.

Peter whistled as he made a new sign.

Think about the selection

1. What does the word *empty* mean in this story?
   a. take out all that is in a thing
   b. a place with nothing in or on it
2. Who do the underlined words in the sentences below refer to?
   a. "People don't know. They say this land is empty."
   b. "We can each make a sign," Jill said.
   c. A bird flew to its nest.
3. What was the problem in this story?
4. How was the problem solved?
5. Did you like the way the problem was solved? Why or why not?

Checkpoint 15

bugs	time	this	girls	ants
park	nest	keep	not	each
use	be	space	no	for

1. Which words have short vowel sounds?
2. Which words have long vowel sounds?
3. Which words have r-controlled vowel sounds?

BENEATH the GRASS

by Ruth H. Gray

I like to peep beneath the grass
To find a thing or two.
Who knows but what a ladybug
Will peep right back at you?

Reprinted from *One
Two*, May 25, 1975.
Copyright © 1975 by
Graded Press.

One day I found a wiggly worm,
Quite long and very brown;
And when I gently touched him
It seemed to me he frowned.

A line of ants were marching forth,
Perhaps to look for food.
What could they find beneath the grass
That ever could be good?

I found a snail almost asleep
All safe inside her shell.
If it were day or night outside
How could she ever tell?

A blade of grass can be a street
For creatures very small;
Maybe a house, a school, a store,
Most anything at all.

Sometimes I find a curious thing
I've never seen before;
A tiny bug can disappear
Right through a tiny door.

Look carefully, walk softly
Wherever you may pass,
So many, many kinds of things
Await beneath the grass!

Strawberries and Monkeys

Billy and his father got on one of the new buses.
They were going to the stores on Green Street.
Billy liked to go shopping with his father.

First they went to a fruit store. Billy and his father
picked out apples, peaches, and strawberries.
At another store they bought some hamburger and
a chicken.

Then Billy and his father went to the store that
Billy liked best. At this store they saw puppies in
the window. They were wagging their tails and
jumping up and down. Inside there were kittens,
birds, and even monkeys.

PET
SHOP

SAM'S
MEAT
MARKET

BAKERY

16: Teach

Soon it was time to go. Billy and his father hurried to the bus stop. In a few minutes they were riding home. Billy and his father talked about their trip all the way home.

Think about skills

» The letters *s, es, ed,* and *ing* are endings. Words to which endings are added are root words. Sometimes a change is made in the root word before an ending is added. **«**

1. What are the root words and endings in the words below?
   a. stores   b. buses
   c. picked   d. jumping
2. How were the root words changed to make the words below?
   a. hurried   b. wagging
   c. liked   d. puppies
3. What are the root words and endings in the words below?
   a. peaches   b. riding   c. shopping
   d. talked   e. going   f. birds
   g. monkeys   h. strawberries

Practice skills

Jane had a job working in a store. She worked there after school.

Each day she cleaned the puppy cages. First she lifted the puppies out of their cages. She carried them carefully to the back room. Then she scrubbed the cages. She put fresh water in their dishes. Then she brought the puppies back. Jane liked her job.

1. What are the endings in the words below?
   a. working   b. cleaned   c. dishes   d. cages
2. What are the root words in the words below?
   a. puppies   b. scrubbed   c. carried

178

INTERESTING HOBBIES

Many people have hobbies. They may collect things as a hobby. You may know someone who collects stamps, little cars, or comic books. On these pages you can see some other things people collect.

Dana Portnoy collects candles. Her candles are shaped like animals, foods, houses, and toys. Dana has also learned how to make candles.

Betty and Tony Rice and their parents collect
picture postcards. They have postcards from all
over the world. Together they sort the postcards
and put them into books.

16: Apply

The Rice family is always looking for picture postcards they don't have. They stopped at this used-book store and found a box of old postcards for sale.

Mr. de la Paz collects dolls. Some of the dolls are over one hundred years old. Many of the dolls have china heads, arms, and legs, and some of the dolls can talk. The dolls have the kinds of clothes people used to wear.

16: Apply

Mr. de la Paz visits stores that sell old furniture,
dishes, and toys to look for more dolls. At this
store he found a beautiful baby doll. Mr. de la Paz
likes to collect dolls because they show him what
some children played with long ago.

Think about the selection

1. What does Dana Portnoy collect?

2. Where did Betty and Tony Rice find some old postcards?

3. What does Mr. de la Paz collect?

4. What is the main idea of the selection?
   a. Dana has learned to make candles.
   b. Some people collect things as a hobby.
   c. Some dolls are over one hundred years old.

Checkpoint 16

1. What are the endings in the words below?
   a. stamps   b. dishes
   c. played   d. looking

2. What are the root words in the words below?
   a. cars   b. stopped   c. hobbies
   d. looking   e. shaped

Sam Makes Cookies

Sam wanted to make some sugar cookies. First he rolled the dough. Next he cut out shapes of funny animals. Then he baked the cookies.

Sam decided to mail a box of the cookies to his grandmother. First he packed the cookies in a box. Next he wrapped the box in brown paper. Then he took the box to the post office.

Think about skills

The order in which things happen can be important. Here is what Sam did first, next, and last to make sugar cookies.

First he rolled the dough.

Next he cut out shapes.

Then he baked the cookies.

1. Was order important? If you said yes, you were right. Sam could not have baked the cookies before he rolled the dough or cut out the shapes.

2. What did Sam do first, next, and last to mail the cookies?

Practice skills

1. What should you do first, next, and last?
   a. Put on your shoes.
   b. Put on your socks.
   c. Tie your shoes.

2. Joel is making chocolate milk. What should he do first, next, and last?
   a. Put the chocolate in the milk.
   b. Stir the chocolate and milk together.
   c. Put some milk in a glass.

3. What probably happened first, next, and last?
   a. Mother opened the mailbox.
   b. Mother read the letter from Joy.
   c. Mother took a letter from Joy out of the mailbox.

Morris had never seen a cow. There were no cows in the building where he lived. There were no cows on the streets. There were no cows on the buses or at the park. There were no cows at all!

Morris had seen pictures of cows. But you can't feel a cow's skin, or watch its tail swish, or listen to it moo in a picture.

"Oh, I wish I could see a cow," Morris said to himself as he walked to school. He held his breath, closed his eyes, and wished with all his might. Then he opened his eyes. When he turned the corner he came face to face with . . .

A COW!

Morris blinked. Could it be real? He closed his eyes.
Then he opened them again.

The cow was still there!

Morris smiled. Then he laughed. "I guess you're the
answer to my wish," Morris said to the cow.

The cow mooed. Then she followed Morris down the street.

Cars stopped. Horns beeped. Everyone stopped to look.

A large truck full of cows came down the street.
Two people were in the front seat.

"There she is!" cried the truck driver. He was pointing
at Morris's cow.

The truck stopped. A woman got out. She led
Morris's cow to the truck.

"I thought that cow was for me," Morris said.

The woman shook her head. "No. The cow belongs on the truck. We're taking these cows to a new farm," she said. "This one climbed off the truck while we were stopped for a red light. I can't imagine why she did such a thing."

Morris smiled a secret smile. He thought about his wish. He knew why the cow had climbed off the truck.

The truck moved away. The cow looked back at Morris.

Morris was almost sure that the cow smiled.

Think about the selection

1. What was Morris's wish?
2. Why did Morris want to see a real cow and not just a picture of a cow?
3. Where did the people want to take the cow?
4. Why do you think the cow climbed off the truck?

Checkpoint 17

1. What happened first, next, and last?
    a. Morris made a wish to see a real cow.
    b. Morris thought the cow smiled at him.
    c. Morris saw a real cow.

2. What happened first, next, and last?
    a. A cow followed Morris down the street.
    b. A cow got off a truck.
    c. Some people put the cow back on the truck.

TRUCKS!

Trucks are used for many different things. Let's look at some different trucks that help people.

This truck carries fruits and vegetables across long distances. The inside of the truck is cold. This keeps the food fresh.

194

Garbage is loaded into the "mouth" of this truck.
Then it is pressed together. Garbage trucks pick up
garbage from homes and stores.

A fire truck takes fire fighters to a fire. A fire truck
carries a machine that pumps and throws water
on a fire. Some fire trucks carry long ladders that
are used to save lives.

This dump truck carries earth from one place and
dumps it in another. The driver moves a lever to
lift the back of the truck. A door opens and the
earth slides out.

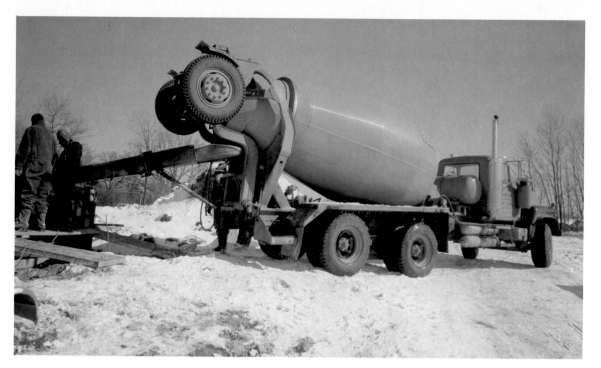

The middle part of this truck goes around and around. Concrete is being mixed inside. Concrete is cement, sand, and water. When this mixture is ready, the back of the truck is opened. Then the concrete pours out. When the concrete dries, it makes a hard surface. Here concrete is being poured to make the bottom floor of a house.

A pickup is a small truck. It is just right for
carrying small machines, furniture, or other small
loads. In what ways have you seen a pickup used?

Think about the selection

1. In what ways do trucks help people?
2. Which truck in the story did you like best? Why?

Pedro Had a Problem

Pedro was getting ready for school. His dog Piper took his shoe. Piper dropped the shoe in her water dish. The shoe was very wet. Pedro couldn't wear it. But Pedro solved his problem. He wore an old pair of shoes.

Think about skills

In many stories there is a problem. Someone usually solves the problem. Pedro had a problem while getting ready for school.

1. What was Pedro's problem?
2. How did Pedro solve the problem?

200

Diane wanted a baseball bat. But she didn't have the money to buy one. Diane got a job taking care of her Uncle Joe's garden. Soon she had the money to buy the baseball bat.

3. What was Diane's problem?
4. How did Diane solve the problem?

Practice skills

Rose wanted to do something nice for her singing teacher. But Rose had no money to buy a gift. Then Rose had an idea. She wrote a song for her teacher. At her next lesson, Rose sang the song for her teacher.

1. What was Rose's problem?
2. How did Rose solve the problem?

The Case of the Sinking Pond

by Robert Quackenbush

Detective Mole got a call from Mrs. Duck. He grabbed his magnifying glass. Then he ran to the pond.

"Detective Mole at your service," he said. But he was talking to a water lily. He couldn't see very well, even with his magnifying glass.

Adapted by permission of Lothrop, Lee & Shepard Company from Chapter 4 of *Detective Mole* by Robert Quackenbush. Copyright © 1976 by Robert Quackenbush. Reprinted by permission.

Mrs. Duck swam toward Detective Mole. "Here I am," she said.

18: Apply

Detective Mole asked Mrs. Duck to tell him her problem.

"The water in my pond is slowly sinking," said Mrs. Duck. "My feet touch the bottom when I swim. I'm sure someone is stealing the water. If this keeps up, my ducklings will never learn to swim."

Detective Mole searched the edge of the pond. He found some footprints. The footprints went across Mrs. Duck's backyard and out the gate.

"Aha!" he said. "I think I've solved this case."

Mrs. Duck and her ducklings followed the footprints with Detective Mole. The footprints led them to Mr. and Mrs. Horse's backyard. They found Mrs. Horse pouring a can of water into some empty bottles.

Detective Mole quietly walked up behind
Mrs. Horse. "I caught you!" he said.

Mrs. Horse jumped in surprise. She dropped
the can and the bottles.

Mrs. Duck was very angry. "Why are you taking water from my pond?" she asked.

"The pond water is so good to drink," Mrs. Horse said. "That's why I'm filling these empty bottles with your pond water. I didn't think you would mind."

"Well!" said Mrs. Duck. "I do mind! My pond is sinking!"

Mrs. Horse said, "Oh, I didn't know that. Please forgive me."

They had always been good friends, so Mrs. Duck forgave Mrs. Horse.

"Besides, it will rain soon," said Detective Mole. "The raindrops will fill your pond again."

Think about the selection

1. What two root words do you see in *backyard* and *raindrops?*

2. "I think I've solved this case," said Detective Mole. What does the word *case* mean in this sentence?
   a. a mystery often cleared up by a detective
   b. a box containing 24 cans of soda pop

3. Find something Detective Mole said in the story. Read it the way you think he said it.

Checkpoint 18

1. What was the problem Detective Mole had to solve?

2. How did he find out Mrs. Horse was taking the water?

3. Detective Mole found out who was taking Mrs. Duck's water. But Mrs. Duck still did not have enough water in her pond. How did Detective Mole think Mrs. Duck's problem would be solved?

Section Two Checkpoint

Word Identification Test

Subtest 1

ⓐ beginning　ⓑ anything ⓒ ladybug　ⓓ DK	4. ⓐ eaten　ⓑ finish ⓒ neighbor　ⓓ DK
1. ⓐ myself　ⓑ mother ⓒ ranches　ⓓ DK	5. ⓐ hungry　ⓑ village ⓒ puppies　ⓓ DK
2. ⓐ country　ⓑ ran ⓒ highest　ⓓ DK	6. ⓐ horse　ⓑ bikes ⓒ house　ⓓ DK
3. ⓐ money　ⓑ liking ⓒ string　ⓓ DK	7. ⓐ storeroom　ⓑ happen ⓒ shopped　ⓓ DK

Possible Word Identification Score: 7　**stop**

Comprehension Tests

Subtest 2

1. Which would you do last? 　ⓐ Get into bed. 　ⓑ Brush your teeth. 　ⓒ Go to sleep. 　ⓓ DK	2. Which would you do last? 　ⓐ Drink the juice. 　ⓑ Pour the juice. 　ⓒ Open the can. 　ⓓ DK

stop

Subtest 3

Jim and Dora went to play outside. They put on boots because it was snowing. They had fun in the snow.

3. Why did Jim and Dora put on boots?
   ⓐ They liked the boots.
   ⓑ The boots were new.
   ⓒ It was snowing.
   ⓓ DK

Laura put on her blue jeans. Then she went out to the barn. Since there was no school on Saturday, she could ride her pony all day.

4. Why could Laura ride all day?
   ⓐ She wore blue jeans.
   ⓑ Her pony was in the barn.
   ⓒ It was Saturday.
   ⓓ DK

stop

Pete couldn't do math.
"I'll never be able to do math.
Not even if I live to be a
hundred."

Pam couldn't read very well.
"I'll never be able to read very
well. Not even if I live to be
a hundred."

Pete said, "Reading is easy.
It's math that's hard."

Pam said, "No, math is
easy. Reading is hard."

Pete said, "Maybe I could help
you with reading."

"And I could help you with
math," Pam said.

Can you guess what happened?
Pete learned math.
Pam learned to read very well.

5. What was Pete's problem?
   ⓐ He didn't like school.
   ⓑ He couldn't do math.
   ⓒ He couldn't read very well.
   ⓓ DK

6. What was Pam's problem?
   ⓐ She couldn't read very well.
   ⓑ She didn't like Pete.
   ⓒ She couldn't do math.
   ⓓ DK

7. How did Pam and Pete solve
   their problems?
   ⓐ Pete read to Pam.
   ⓑ They helped each other.
   ⓒ Pam did Pete's math.
   ⓓ DK

8. Could this story really have
   happened?
   ⓐ Yes   ⓑ No   ⓒ DK

go on

Chair folded his legs and leaned against the wall. "Wow! First the children climbed all over me. Then they made a train of me. I thought they'd never go to bed."

Table stretched out three legs. He propped his head on the fourth one. "I couldn't stand up another minute. They ran around me until I was dizzy."

Clock looked down at Chair and Table. "Shame on you," she ticked. "If I acted the way you are, time would stop. Think what would happen. Morning wouldn't come. You'd be stuck just the way you are. The children never would be back."

Chair looked at Table. Table looked at Chair. "I guess the children really aren't that bad, after all," they said.

9. Could this story really have happened?
   ⓐ Yes   ⓑ No   ⓒ DK

10. How did Table and Chair feel at the end of the day?
    ⓐ happy   ⓑ tired
    ⓒ cold   ⓓ DK

11. What did the children make of Chair?
    ⓐ a table   ⓑ a ship
    ⓒ a train   ⓓ DK

12. What did the children do to Table?
    ⓐ broke one of his legs
    ⓑ stretched his legs
    ⓒ made him dizzy
    ⓓ DK

Possible Comprehension Score: 12   **stop**

Study and Research Test

Subtest 5

boxer 1. a man who boxes. 2. a kind of dog.

brook a small stream.

burn 1. be on fire; be very hot. 2. a sore caused by heat.

burro a kind of small donkey.

burrow a hole in the ground.

button 1. a knob or object on clothing to hold edges closed. 2. a knob to take hold of, push, or turn. See the picture.

boxer

buzz

button 2.

1. What are the guide words?
   ⓐ **boxer** and **buzz**
   ⓑ **boxer** and **button**
   ⓒ **bother** and **burn**
   ⓓ DK

2. Which word could be on this page?
   ⓐ born   ⓑ broke
   ⓒ by   ⓓ DK

3. Which definition of **burn** is used in this sentence?
   Sara has a burn on her arm.
   ⓐ 1   ⓑ 2   ⓒ DK

4. What is a **burro?**
   ⓐ an animal
   ⓑ a hole
   ⓒ DK

5. Which definition of **button** is pictured?
   ⓐ 1   ⓑ 2   ⓒ DK

Possible Study and Research Score: 5   stop

ICE CREAM

by Arnold Lobel

One hot summer day Frog and Toad were fishing
in the pond.

"I wish we had some sweet, cold ice cream," said
Frog.

"What a good idea," said Toad. "Wait right here,
Frog. I will be back soon."

Toad went to the store. He bought two big ice-cream cones.

Toad licked one of the cones.

"Frog likes chocolate best," said Toad. "And so do I."

Toad walked along the path. A large, soft drop of chocolate ice cream slipped down his arm.

"This ice cream is melting in the sun," said Toad.

Toad walked faster. Many drops of melting ice cream flew through the air. They fell down on Toad's head.

"I must hurry back to Frog!" he cried.

219

More and more of the ice cream was melting. It dropped down on Toad's jacket. It splattered on his pants and on his feet.

"Where is the path?" cried Toad. "I cannot see."

Frog sat by the pond waiting for Toad. A mouse ran by.

"I just saw something awful!" cried the mouse. "It was big and brown!"

"Something covered with sticks and leaves is moving this way!" cried a squirrel.

"Here comes a thing with horns!" shouted a rabbit. "Run for your life!"

"What can it be?" asked Frog.

Frog hid behind a rock. He saw the thing coming.
It was big and brown. It was covered with sticks
and leaves. It had two horns.

"Frog," cried the thing. "Where are you?"

"My goodness!" said Frog. "That thing is Toad!"

Toad fell into the pond. He sank to the bottom
and came up again.

"Oh, no," said Toad. "All of our sweet, cold ice
cream has washed away."

"Never mind," said Frog. "I know what we can do."

Frog and Toad quickly ran back to the store. Then they sat in the shade of a large tree and ate their chocolate ice-cream cones together.

Glossary

bill

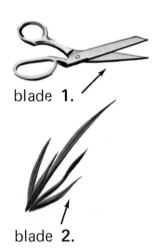

blade 1.

blade 2.

blue ribbon

A   a

al pha bet i cal put in the order of the alphabet: *The names were in alphabetical order.*

au di ence 1. people gathered in one place to hear or see something: *The audience liked the circus.* 2. any people who can see or hear: *a radio audience, a TV audience.* **au di enc es.**

B   b

bal ance 1. being steady; not falling over: *He lost his balance and fell.* 2. keep or put in a steady position: *She could balance the jar on her head.* **bal anced, bal anc ing.**

bill the mouth of a bird. See the picture. **bills.**

blade 1. the cutting part of a knife or scissors: *This knife has a sharp blade.* 2. a leaf of grass. See the pictures. **blades.**

blink shut and open the eyes very fast: *She blinked at the bright light.* **blinked, blink ing.**

blue rib bon a first prize given to the winner of a game or contest: *She won the race and got a blue ribbon. He came in second and got a red ribbon.* See the picture. **blue rib bons.**

228

boost a push or shove that helps a person move up: *The woman gave the boy a boost over the fence.* **boosts.**

bronze 1. a brown metal made of copper and tin. 2. made of this metal: *She won a bronze medal in the race.*

C   c

car toon a picture that shows something funny: The cartoon of the bear made us laugh. See the picture. **car toons.**

cen ti pede a small animal with many pairs of legs. See the picture. **cen ti pedes.**

chi na dishes, vases, or other things made of clay baked in a special way: *We bought a new set of china.*

claw a sharp nail on the foot of a bird or an animal. See the pictures. **claws.**

cous in the son or daughter of an uncle or aunt. **cous ins.**

crea ture any living person or animal. **crea tures.**

crumb a tiny bit broken from something bigger: *A crumb of bread fell on the floor.* **crumbs.**

cu ri ous 1. wanting to know: *The curious kitten poked its nose into the basket.* 2. strange; odd: *I found a curious old hat.*

cartoon

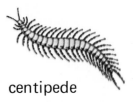

centipede

claws of a bird

claws of an animal

229

D d

dan ger ous likely to cause harm; not safe.

def i ni tion the words that tell what something is or what a word means. **def i ni tions.**

de tec tive a person who finds information secretly in order to solve a problem. **de tec tives.**

dis cov er find out; see for the first time: *We discovered a bird's nest in the tree.* **dis cov ered, dis cov er ing.**

dough a mixture used to make bread, pies, cakes, and cookies: *He made dough for cookies with flour, milk, eggs, and sugar.* **doughs.**

drag on in stories, an animal that breathes fire. See the picture. **drag ons.**

dragon

E e

emp ty 1. with nothing in it: *The cookie jar was empty.* 2. to pour out or take out all that is in a thing: *They emptied their cups.* 3. to flow out: *The river empties into the ocean.* **emp tied, emp ty ing.**

enor mous very, very large.

en try 1. the act of going into a place: *She made her entry through the window.* 2. a place by which to enter: *Leave your boots in the entry.* See the picture. 3. a word and how it is explained in a dictionary or glossary: *Look up an entry in this book.* **en tries.**

entry 2.

F   f

fair a show or sale of farm animals, clothes, and baked and canned food. **fairs.**

flour the fine powder made of ground-up grain such as wheat or corn and used in cooking. **flours.**

G   g

glide to move along in a smooth or even way: *The skater glides over the ice*. **glid ed, glid ing.**

skaters gliding
on ice

H   h

ham ster an animal that looks like a mouse, but is bigger. See the picture. **ham sters.**

hob by something a person likes to do for fun: *His hobby is bike riding*. **hob bies.**

hol i day a day when you do not work or go to school; a day for having fun. **hol i days.**

house keep er a person who takes care of a home and does housework. **house keep ers.**

hamster

231

ladybug

lever **1.**

magnifying glass

L   l

la dy bug a small, red beetle with black spots. See the picture. **la dy bugs.**

lean 1. stand slanting or bent: *Snow made the bushes lean over to the ground.* 2. rest upon something: *Lean on the wall.* **leaned, lean ing.**

led showed the way by going along with or in front of: *She led the horses to the river.*

lev er 1. a bar used to move something heavy. See the picture. 2. a bar in a machine that acts to move parts of the machine: *Pulling this lever makes the back of the truck go up.* **lev ers.**

li brary 1. a group of books: *I started my library with three books.* 2. a room or building where books are kept. **li brar ies.**

lone ly 1. feeling alone and wanting to be with someone: *The boy felt lonely when he went to camp.* 2. without many people around: *The street was lonely at night.* **lone li er, lone li est.**

M   m

mag ni fy ing glass a glass that makes things look larger. See the picture. **mag ni fy ing glass es.**

make - be lieve pretend; not real: *Dragons are make-believe creatures.*

mam mal a kind of animal that feeds milk to its young. **mam mals.**

may or person in charge of a city government. **may ors.**

med i cine something to help a sick person get well. **med i cines.**

mum ble to talk with lips partly closed: *You won't understand what I say if I mumble.* **mum bled, mum bling.**

P   p

par a graph a group of sentences about the same idea. **par a graphs.**

puz zle 1. a hard problem. 2. a problem or game done for fun: *He was working a puzzle.* See the picture. 3. not able to understand something: *How the mouse got in puzzled us.* **puz zles; puz zled, puz zling.**

puzzle 2.

R   r

rain bow part of a circle of colors sometimes seen in the sky when the sun shines during a rain. See the picture. **rain bows.**

rainbow

rattle
_____

shore

fish scales

scrubbing a car

shore

rat tle 1. make short, sharp sounds: *The door rattled.* 2. short, sharp sounds: *We heard the rattle of the dishes.* **rat tled, rat tling.**

rea son why something happens or why someone does something: *Tell me your reason for going.* **rea sons.**

rep tile a kind of animal that has scales: *Snakes and turtles are reptiles.* **rep tiles.**

S s

scale one of the thin, hard pieces that cover fish and snakes. See the picture. **scales.**

sched ule a list: *A timetable is a schedule that shows when trains arrive and leave.* **sched ules.**

scrub rub hard; wash or clean by rubbing. See the picture. **scrubbed, scrub bing.**

shed 1. pour out; let flow: *The baby shed tears.* 2. throw off: *The snake shed its skin.* **shed, shed ding.**

shore land at the edge of an ocean or lake. See the picture. **shores.**

sink 1. go down slowly; go lower and lower: *The sun sinks in the sky.* **2.** go under: *The ship is sinking.* **3.** a small tub with a drain: *They washed their hands in the sink.* See the picture. **sank** or **sunk, sunk, sink ing; sinks.**

slam shut with a noise: *Don't slam the door!* **slammed, slam ming.**

solve find the answer to: *Mother solved the mystery.* **solved, solv ing.**

stage the raised platform in a theater: *We saw a play on the stage at our school.* See the picture. **stag es.**

stare 1. look for a long time with the eyes wide open: *Don't stare at people.* **2.** a long look. **stared, star ing; stares.**

stat ue something carved from stone or wood. See the picture. **stat ues.**

stilts a pair of poles used to walk on. See the picture.

stuck 1. pushed into with a pointed tool: *I stuck my finger with a needle.* **2.** put; placed: *He stuck a pencil in his pocket.* **3.** held very tight: *It was stuck in the mud.*

sink 3.

stage

statue

girl walking on stilts

T   t

track 1.

track 2.

train 1.

trophy

track 1. rails for trains to run on: *Look before you cross the railroad tracks.* 2. a mark left: *There were tire tracks in the snow.* See the pictures. 3. follow by marks or smell: *The dog tracked the rabbit into the woods.* 4. make marks on: *Don't track mud on the floor.* **tracks; tracked, track ing.**

train 1. a line of railroad cars that move together: *I see the train coming down the track.* See the picture. 2. bring up; teach: *She trained her dog.* **trains; trained, train ing.**

tro phy a prize, usually a statue or cup, given to the winner of a race or contest. See the picture. **tro phies.**

tum ble 1. to fall: *The child tumbled down the stairs.* 2. a fall: *The tumble hurt him.* **tum bled, tum bling; tum bles.**

V   v

va ca tion time out of school or away from work: *We took a vacation last week.* **va ca tions.**

vil lage a place people live, smaller than a town. **vil lag es.**

W w

webbed having the toes held together by a piece of skin: *Ducks have webbed feet*. See the picture.

whis tle 1. make a clear, sharp sound with your lips: *I whistled for my dog*. 2. the sound made by whistling. 3. a thing that makes a whistling sound. See the picture. 4. blow an instrument that makes whistling sounds. **whis tled, whis tling; whis tles.**

duck's webbed feet

whistle 1.

whistle 3.

237

Word List

The following high-frequency words (words that appear on recognized word lists) have been read enough times in this and previous pupils' texts in *Basics in Reading* to reach mastery by the end of this book. Pupils will be able to recognize both the root word and the root word with these endings and spelling changes: *s, es, ed, ing, 's, er, est, en;* final consonant doubled, final *e* dropped, final *y* changed to *i.*

The page number printed after each word shows the first appearance in this book. For a cumulative list of high-frequency words see the Teacher's Edition for *Daisy Days.*

above 37
across 143
again 15
along 25
also 69
always 181
answer 60
around 158
away 11

barn 163
basket 49
because 91
bee 109
been 13
before 26
began 82
believe 151
belong 192
below 8
bent 49
beside 121

best 58
block 56
bought 134
branch 41
brother 19
buy 61

cage 18
car 9
carry 40
case 39
caught 28
chair 8
change 141
chase 102
city 9
climb 192
close 9
coat 56
country 30
cry 11

dear 127
decide 26
desk 117
didn't 18
drink 95
drop 205

ear 75
else 156
empty 164
even 92
ever 35
eye 32

fair 81
family 69
far 57
fat 81
feel 122
feet 124
felt 122
field 49

final 79
fine 30
finger 75
five 18
floor 31
follow 21
food 30
fur 41

garden 81
gate 56
give 55
grass 24
gray 88
ground 25
group 37
guess 9

hair 41
hand 42
hang 146
hard 58

head 74
hear 16
hello 59
hid 223
high 47
hit 9
hole 31
honey 126
hop 78
horn 161
hurry 62

I'll 14
inside 84
its 164

job 88

keep 194
key 116
knew 21
know 19

ladder 92
lady 12
land 80
laugh 10
leap 153
learn 39
left 56
light 146
lost 119

mark 88
may 49

meet 37
middle 16
might 24
money 61
most 42
mouse 30
move 25
much 35

name 28
need 18
nest 30
never 15
new 37
nice 17
night 11
nod 29
note 129

off 47
old 140
once 28
order 87
owl 39

pen 75
person 93
pie 30
pile 20
pin 49
place 167
plan 17
plant 30
please 29
problem 170

question 16

raccoon 25
reach 50
ready 47
real 151
roll 185

sat 17
seen 78
shape 37
should 146
shout 29
show 37
side 20
sign 71
sister 15
sit 126
sleep 42
smile 140
solve 170
splash 78
squirrel 47
start 17
stone 60
stop 12
store 37
street 20
sun 9
sure 13
surprise 15
sweet 215

table 118
talk 150

tap 146
teach 15
telephone 47
than 78
thank 29
their 37
thought 62
through 31
today 39
toe 24
together 8
top 60
touch 41
toy 151
track 19
train 40
trick 88

upon 153
us 28

village 28

wag 142
wear 42
well 52
while 17
wing 42
winter 47
wise 48
wish 188
wolf 107
wrote 129

yes 16

A separate group of words considered technical in this program appears below. Pupils will be able to recognize these terms.